SCHOOL

OF

ADVANCED
PIANO PLAYING

(EXERCISES)

BY

RAFAEL JOSEFFY

Ed. 158

G. SCHIRMER, Inc.

DISTRIBUTED BY

HAL•LEONARD®
CORPORATION

7777 W. BLUEMOUND RD. P.O. BOX 13819 MILWAUKEE, WI 53213

CONTENTS

INHALTSVERZEICHNIS

Five-finger Exercises.   1.   Fünffingerübungen.

RAFAEL JOSEFFY.

a. **I.**

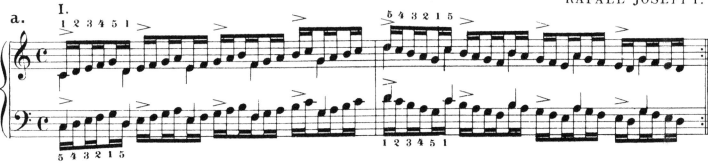

II.

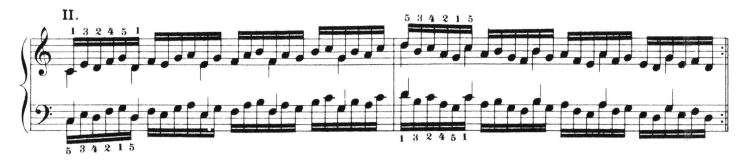

III.

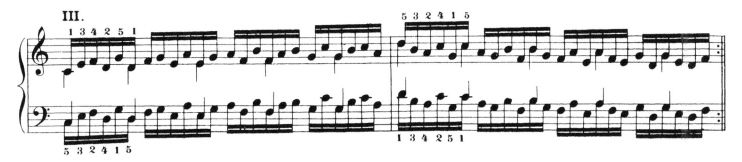

IV.

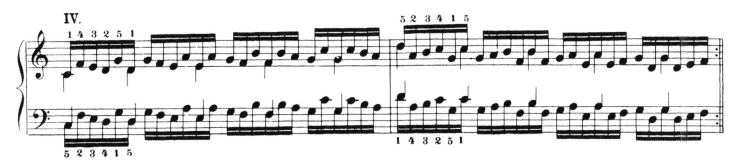

V.

16268

simile

etc.

Through all the keys.
Durch alle **Tonarten.**

b.

II.

III.

IV.

V.

c.

2.

Three-finger Exercises
with Supporting Finger.

Dreifingerübungen
mit Stützfinger.

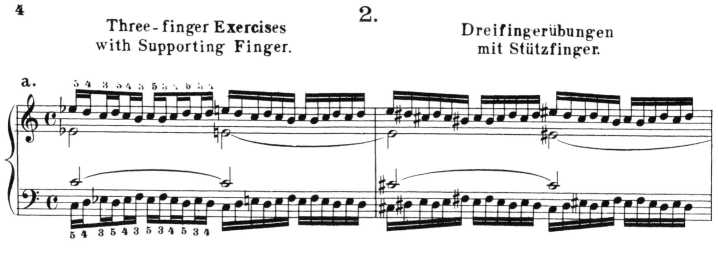

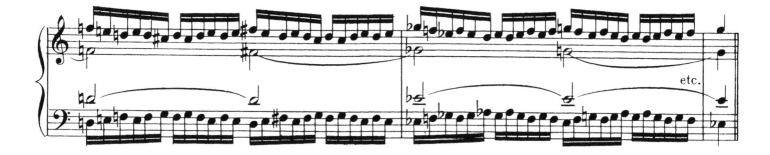

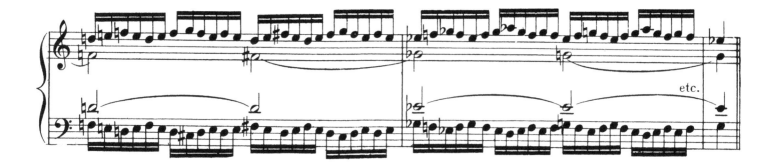

a.

b.

Each hand alone.
Jede Hand allein.

*) Do not strike the little notes, but bring the thumb over them.

16268

*) Die *kleinen* Noten werden nicht angeschlagen.

8

Scale-exercises. | Scalenübungen.

a.

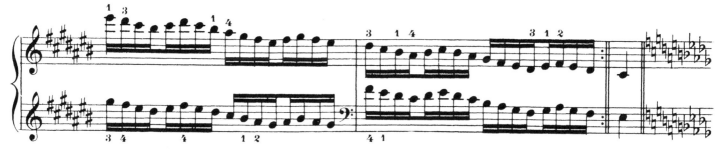

Through all the keys.
Durch alle Tonarten.

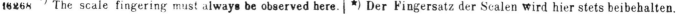

16268 *) The scale fingering must always be observed here. | *) Der Fingersatz der Scalen wird hier stets beibehalten.

b.

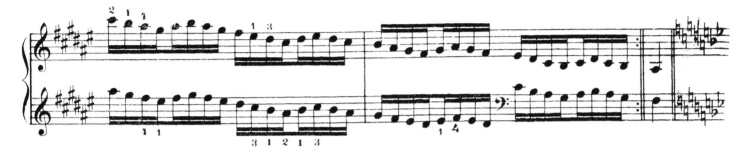

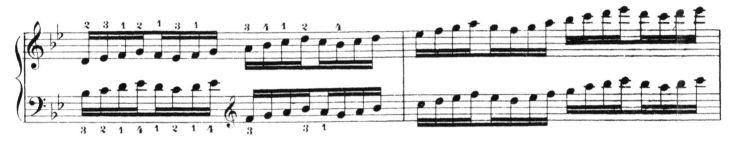

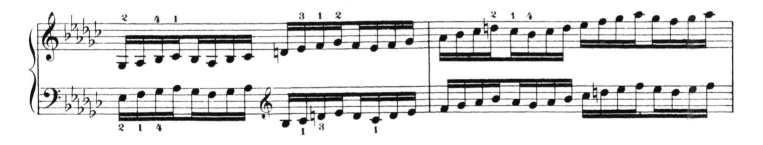

etc.

16268

a.

legato

etc.

b. *legato*

*)   Or right hand alone.
**) Or left hand alone.

*)   oder rechte Hand allein.
**) oder linke Hand allein.

16268

a.

also:
auch:

etc.

b.

etc.

a.

etc.

b.

etc.

*) Wie vorher.

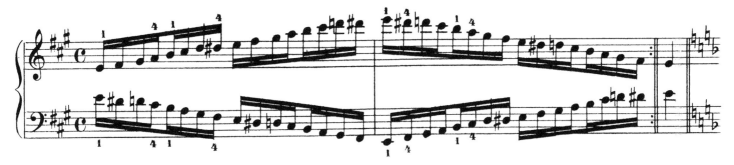

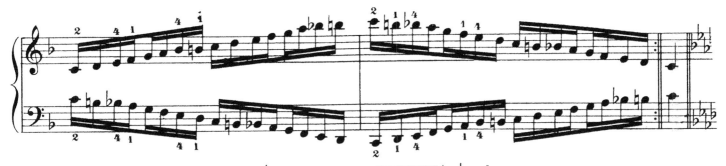

16268

4.

Trills.　　　　　　　　　　　Triller.

I.

a. Moderato.

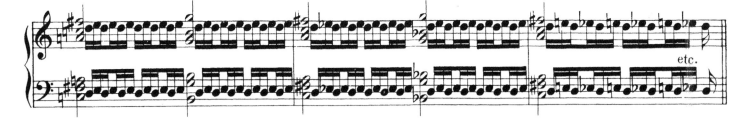

etc.

b. Allegro.

etc

c.

etc

16268

III.

a. Moderato.

b. Allegro.

c.

Arpeggios.

5.

I.

Arpeggien.

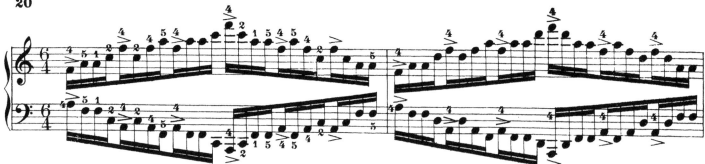

a.

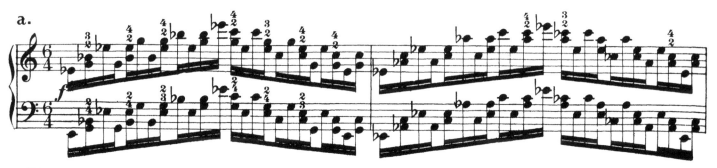

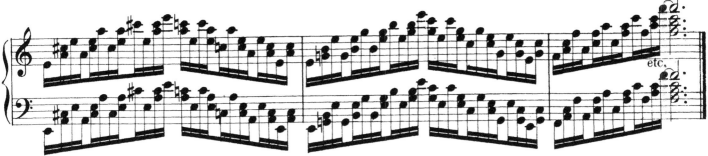

b.

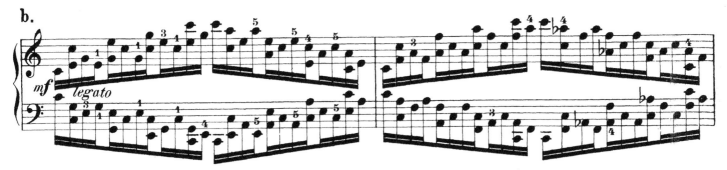

22

a. Moderato.

b. Allegro.

Andante.

Allegro.

a.

16268

b.

In this first exercise hold each finger down firmly.

II.

Bei der ersten Übung jeden Finger fest liegen lassen.

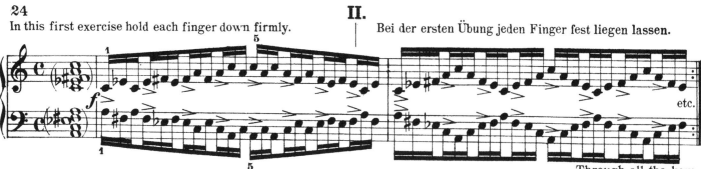

etc.

Through all the keys.
Durch alle Tonarten.

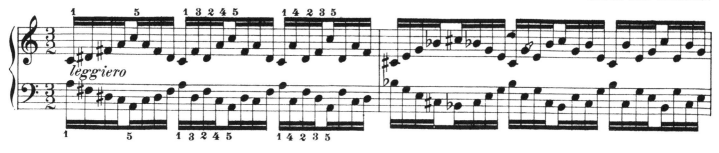

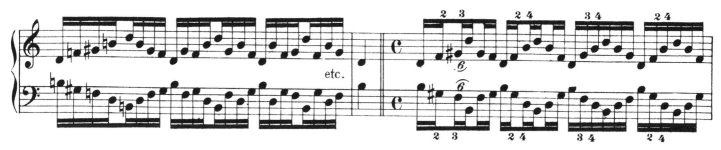

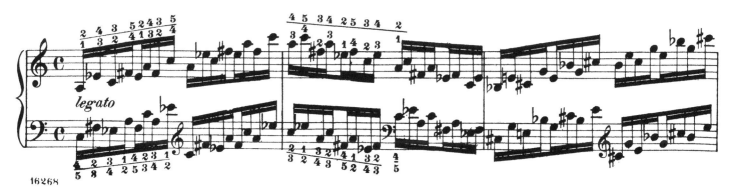

a.

26

b.

c.

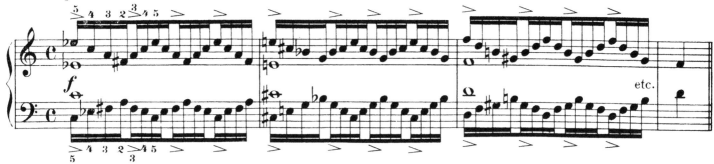

etc.

etc.

etc.

etc.

etc.

etc.

16268

a.

b.

a.

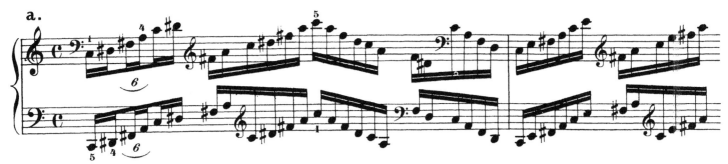

b.

a.

b.

III.

In this first exercise hold each finger down firmly.   In der ersten Übung jeden Finger fest liegen lassen.

Through all the keys.
Durch alle Tonarten.

Through all the keys.
Durch alle Tonarten.

a.

b.

30

a.

b.

a.

b.

16268

a.

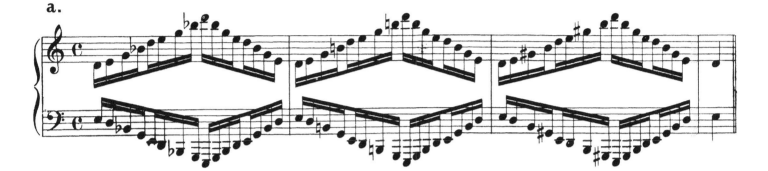

b.

a.

b.

32

IV.

Black keys only.   Obertasten allein.

a.

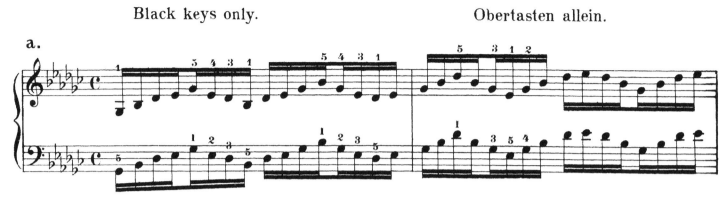

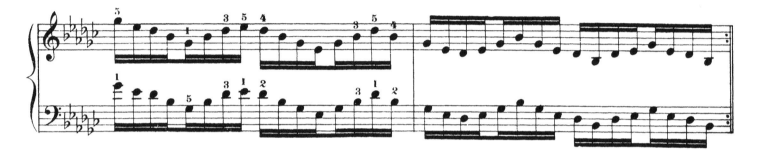

b.

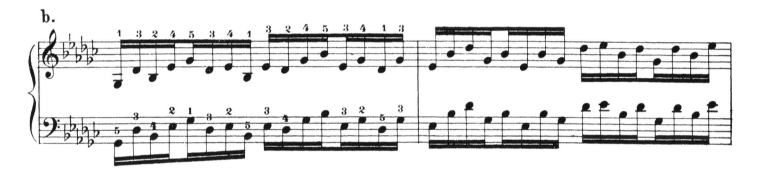

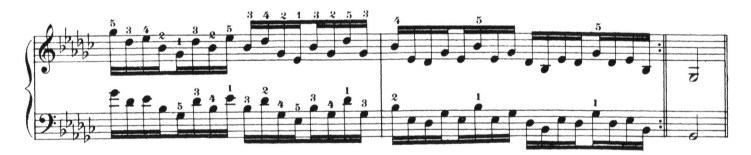

a.

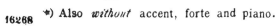

16268 *) Also *without* accent, forte and piano.   *) Auch ohne Accent, forte and piano.

b.

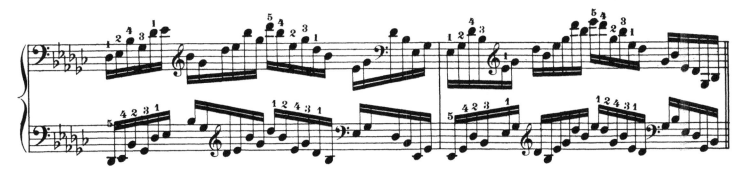

6.

Thirds.   Terzen.

a. At beginning, each group 4 times. | Anfangs jedes Viertel 4 mal.

legato

b. ⁵₃ ⁴₂

²₄ ³₅

a.

b.

a.

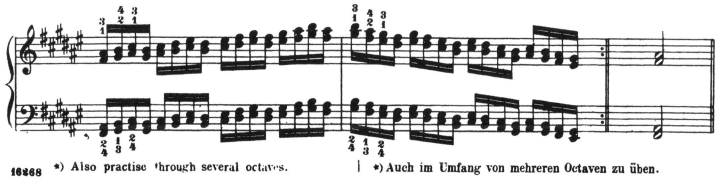

*) Also practise through several octaves.   *) Auch im Umfang von mehreren Octaven zu üben.

Through all the keys.
Durch alle Tonarten.

b.

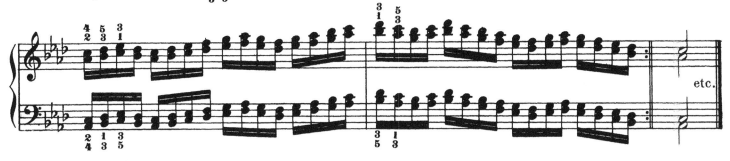

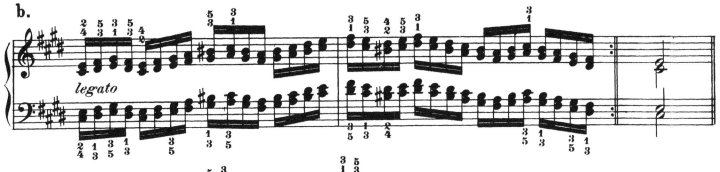

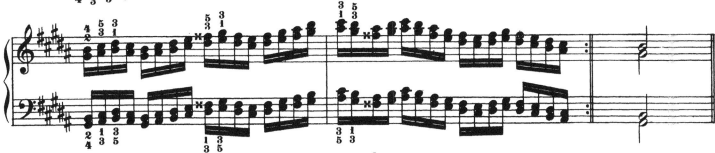

etc.

Each hand alone. Jede Hand allein.

a.

legatissimo

38

a.

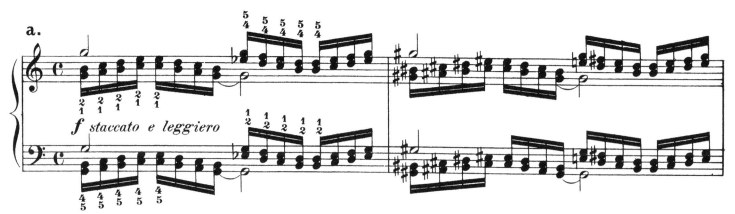

b.

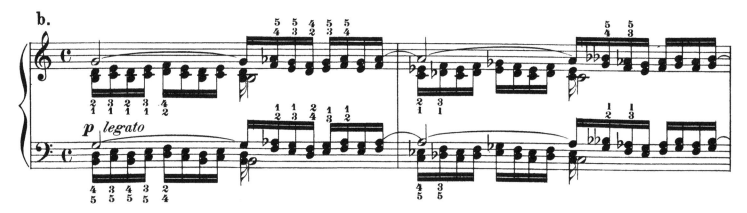

Moderato.

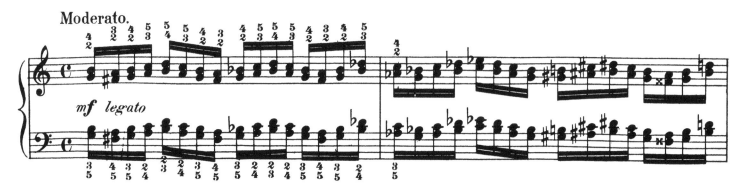

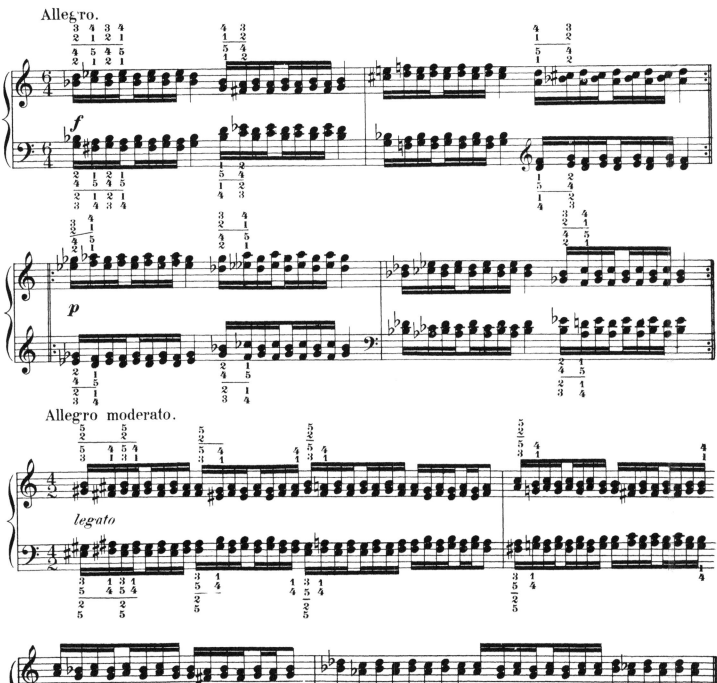

Allegro.

Allegro moderato.

7.

Sixths.   Sexten.

Through all the keys.
Durch alle Tonarten.

b.

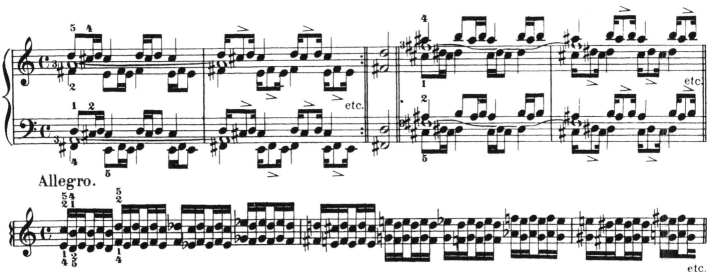

Allegro.

Left hand two octaves lower.
Die linke Hand zwei Octaven tiefer.

Moderato.
a.

b.

16268

a.

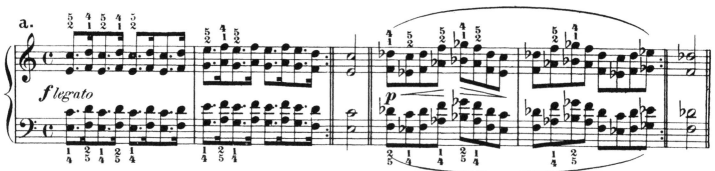

b.

a. Allegro

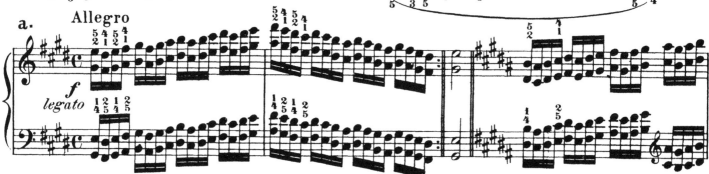

Through all the keys. Durch alle Tonarten.

b.

etc.

Each hand alone.
Jede Hand allein.

a.

b.

Octaves.   8.   Octaven.

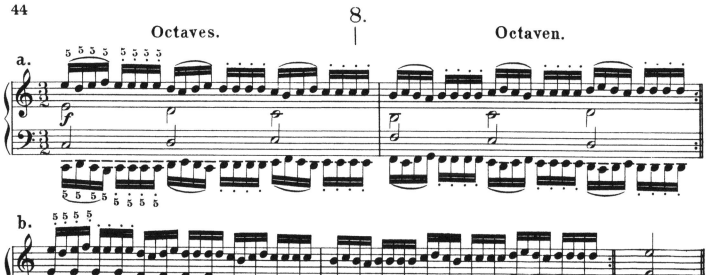

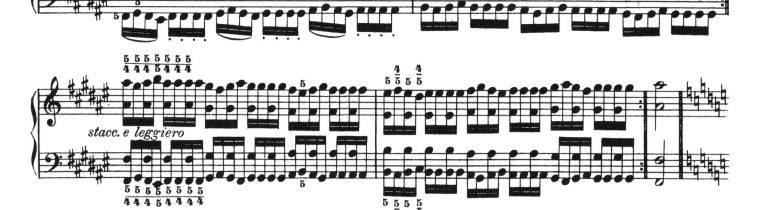

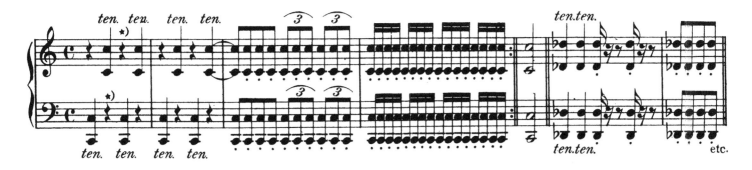

Through all the keys.
Durch alle Tonarten.

16268

*) Wrist-stroke. Throw back the hand quickly before the rest.

Hold the arm easily.

**) After sufficient preparation, practise also with the 4th finger on the white keys and the 3d finger on the black keys.

Equally adapted for the study of "broken" octaves.

*) Anschlag vom Handgelenk – die Hand wird vor der Pause rasch emporgeschnellt.

Die Haltung des Armes ungezwungen.

**) Nach genügender Vorbereitung, auch mit dem 4ten Finger auf der weissen und dem 3ten auf der Obertaste zu üben.

Ebenso zum Studium der „gebrochenen" Oktaven geeignet.

a.

etc.

b.

etc.

a.

etc.

b.

etc.

etc.

etc.

etc.

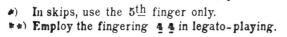
*) In skips, use the 5th finger only.
**) Employ the fingering 4 4 in legato-playing.

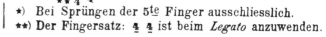
*) Bei Sprüngen der 5te Finger ausschliesslich.
**) Der Fingersatz: 4 4 ist beim *Legato* anzuwenden.

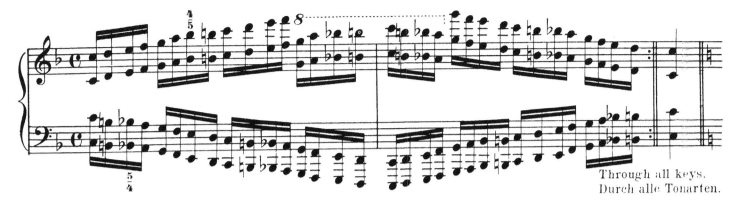

Through all keys.
Durch alle Tonarten.

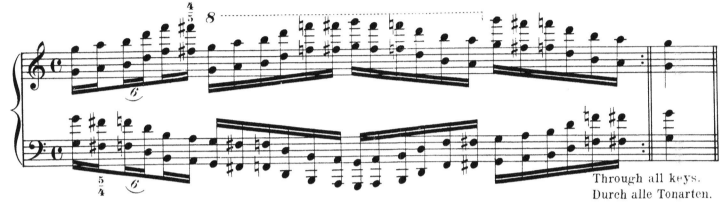

Through all keys.
Durch alle Tonarten.

a.

b.

etc.

etc.

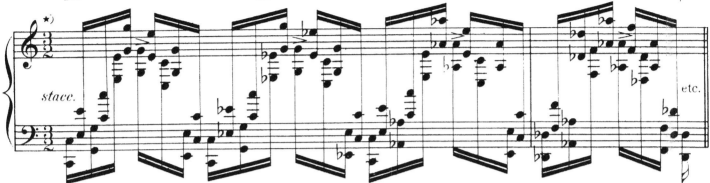

a.

b.

16268

50

Legato.

Through all keys.
Durch alle Tonarten.

legato sempre

legato

staccato

b.

etc. staccato

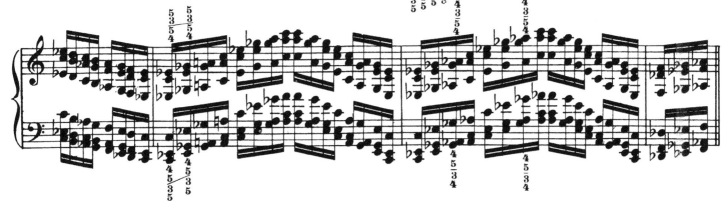

legato

etc. legatissimo

etc.

Chromatic Exercises.

9.

Right hand alone. Rechte Hand allein.

Left hand alone. Linke Hand allein.

54

a.

b.

Allegro moderato.

Right hand alone. Rechte Hand allein.
Allegro.

Left hand alone. Linke Hand allein.

16268

10.

Changing Fingers on One Key (Repetitions). Fingerwechsel auf einer Taste.

*) Strike the tied notes *silently*, but with force. | *) Die gebundenen Noten sind lautlos doch kräftig Anzuschlagen.

II.

Left hand an octave lower.   Linke Hand eine Octave tiefer.

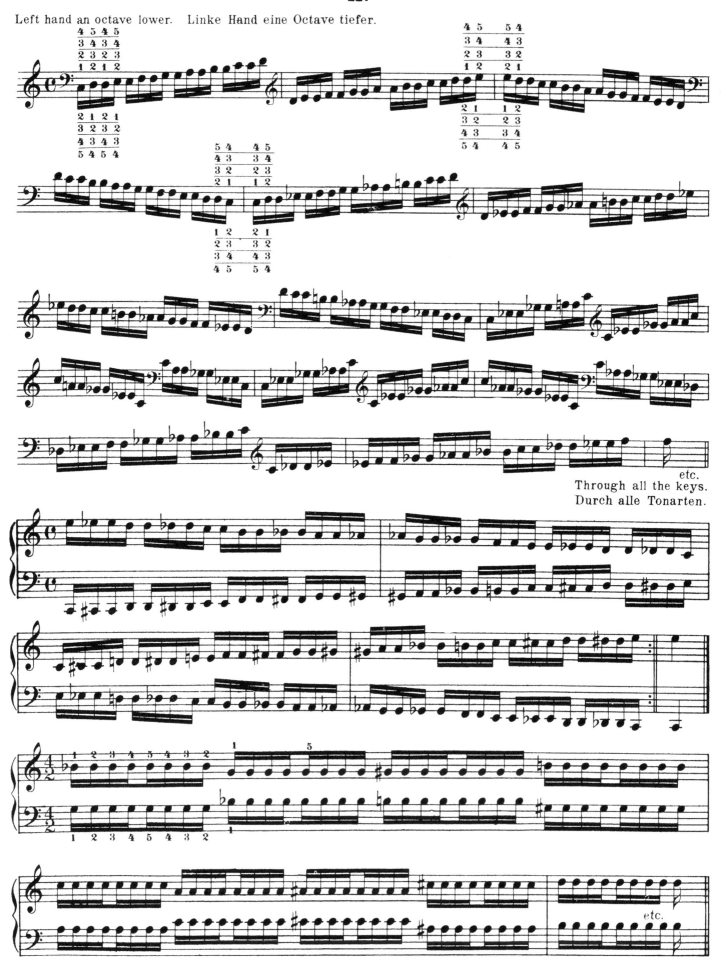

etc.
Through all the keys.
Durch alle Tonarten.

62

Allegro.

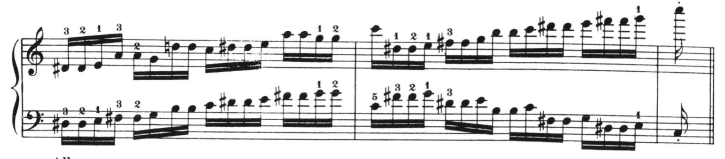

Allegro.

Moderato.

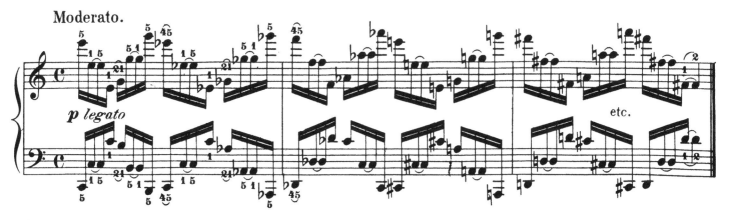

16268

etc.

etc.

Through all the keys.
Durch alle Tonarten.

etc.

etc.

etc.

a.

etc.

16268

etc.

b.

etc.

Allegro.

leggiero

etc.

11.

Repetitions without Changing Fingers.
(Light Wrist-work.)

Repetitionen ohne Fingerwechsel.
(Handgelenk.)

12.

For Developing the Independence and Strength of the Fingers. (Paired Notes.) | Zur Entwicklung der Selbständigkeit und Kraft der Finger. (Doppelgriffe.)

*) Each measure 4 times.　　　　*) Jeder Takt 4 mal.

69

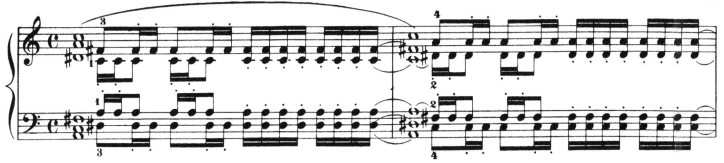

etc.

Through all the keys.
Durch alle Tonarten.

a.

etc.

b.

etc.

etc.

16268

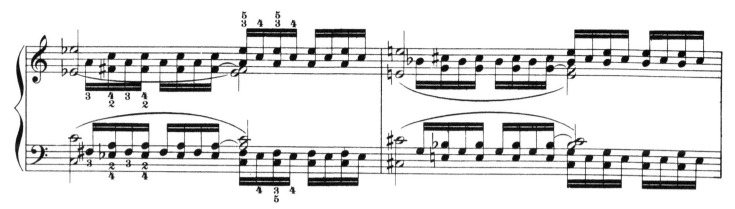

a.

b.

a. Legato.

b.

Moderato.

a.

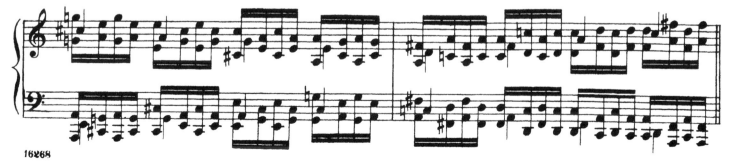

Allegro.

Allegro.

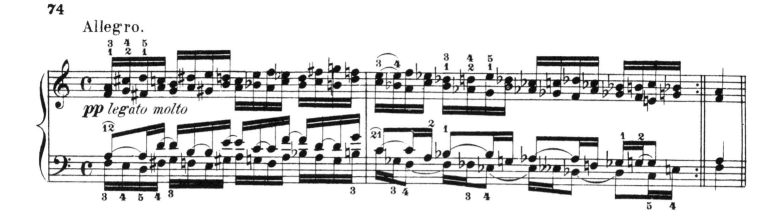

Allegro.

13.

Chords. Wrist-exercises. | Akkorde. Handgelenkübungen.

staccato e leggiero

Through all the keys.
Durch alle Tonarten.

etc.

a.

ten. ten. ten. ten.

f

etc.

ten. ten. ten. ten.

b.

etc.

*)

p

etc.

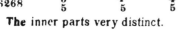

The inner parts very distinct. | *) Die Mittelstimmen sehr deutlich.

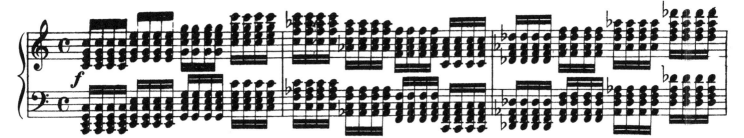

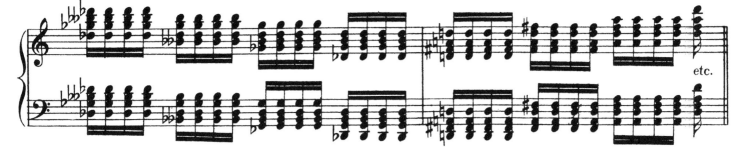

etc.

Allegro.

etc.

Allegro moderato.

Allegro.

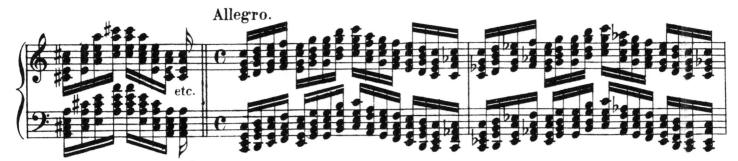

etc.

etc.

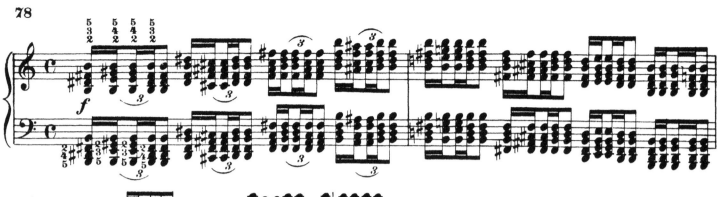

a.

b.

Allegro.

*) The inner parts very distinct.   *) Die Mittelstimmen sehr deutlich.

14.

Alternation and Interlacing
of the Hands.

Ablösen und Ineinandergreifen
der Hände.

Through several keys.
Durch mehrere Tonarten.

etc.

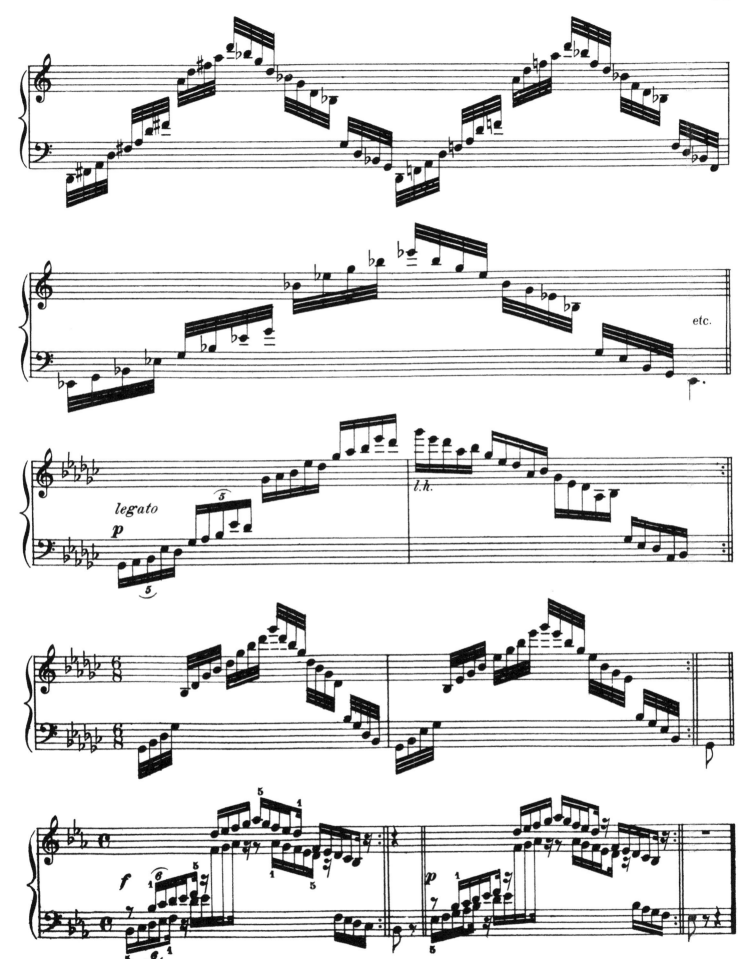

a.

b.

a. Moderato.

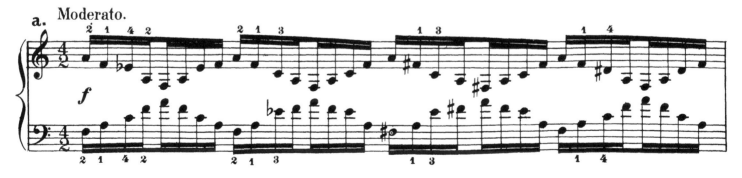

etc.

Più mosso.

b.

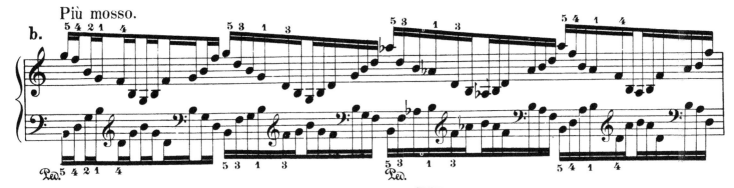

etc.

Andante. *legato*

p tranquillo

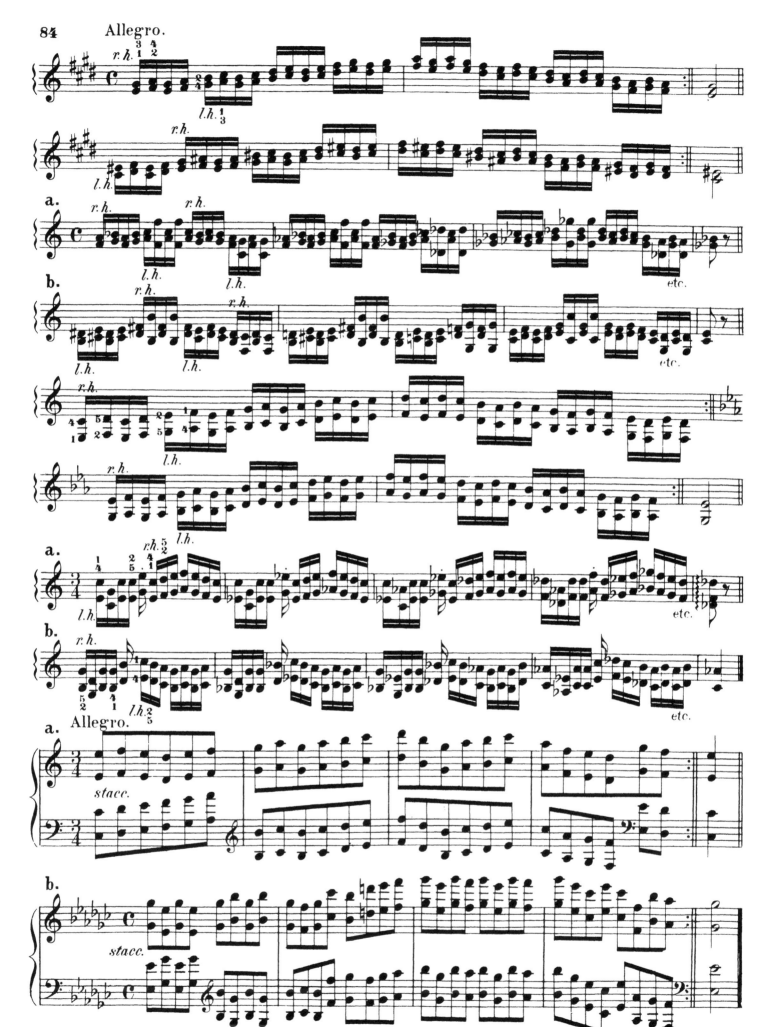

15.

Various Styles of Touch.   Verschiedene Anschlagsarten.

All tones of equal force.
Stimmen gleich stark.

Through all keys.
Durch alle Tonarten.

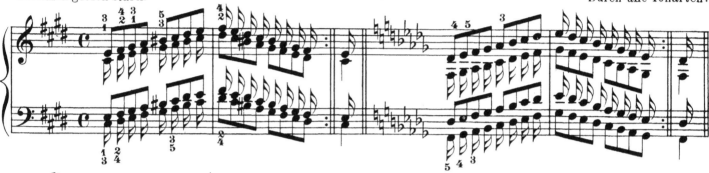

etc

a.

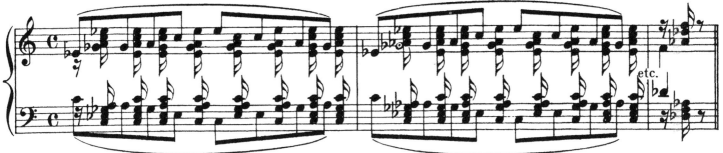

b.

Through all the keys.
Durch alle Tonarten.

16268

16.

Thumb-exercises. | Daumen-Übungen.

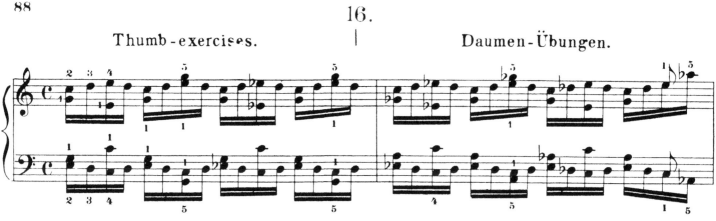

Allegro. Right hand alone. Rechte Hand allein.

Left hand alone. Linke Hand allein.

Allegro.

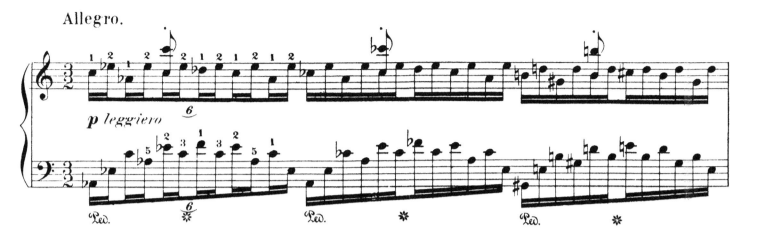

Allegro molto.

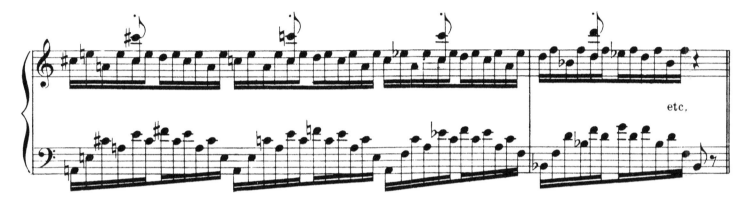

17.

Sliding from the Black Keys.   Herabgleiten von den Obertasten.

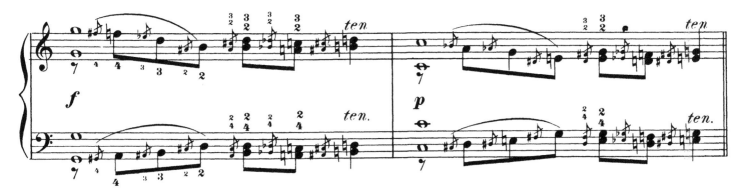

18.

The Glissando

Glissando

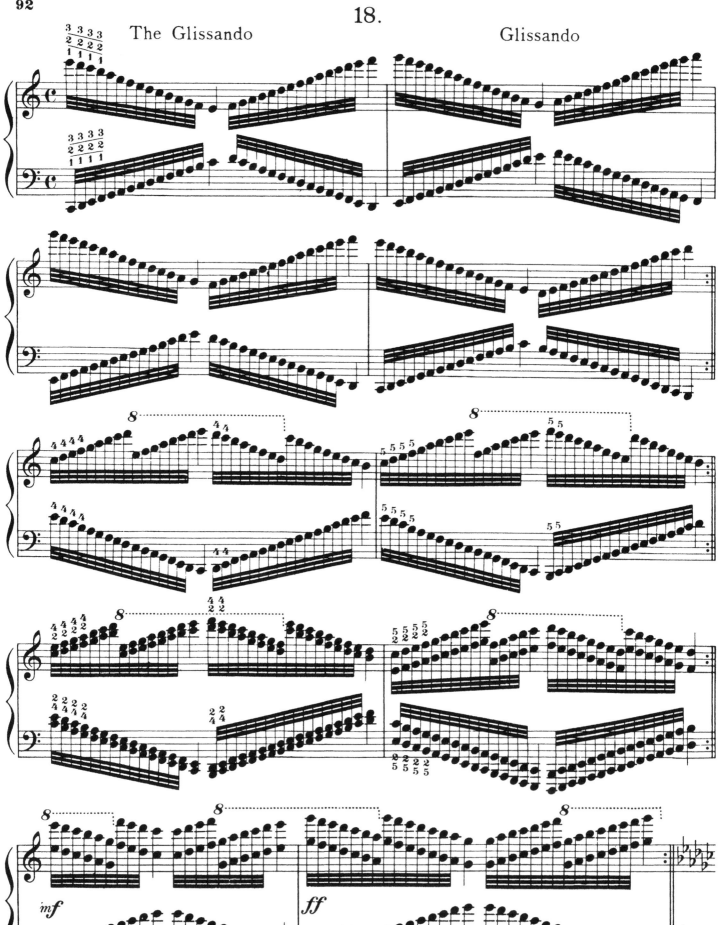

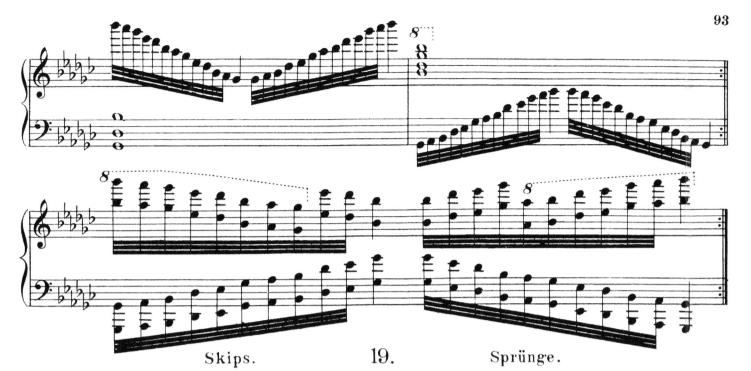

Skips. **19.** Sprünge.

staccato e leggiero

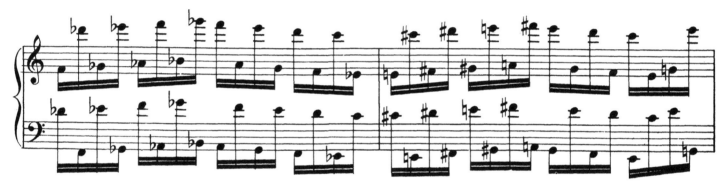

b.

staccato

etc.

etc.

etc.

20.

Embellishments.   Verzierungen.

a.

b.

Moderato.

Andante.

Andante tranquillo.

a.

Through all keys.

Durch alle Tonarten.

b.

etc.

Allegro.

etc.

etc.

etc.

97

16268

Allegretto.

Allegro.

Moderato.

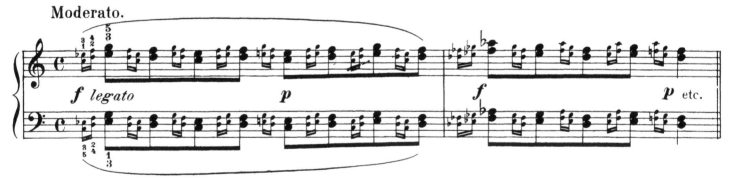

Allegro.

a.

legato

b.

Allegro.

a.

b. Moderato.

legato

16268

21.

Extended Chords and Figures.   Übungen in weiter Lage.

Through all keys.
Durch alle Tonarten.

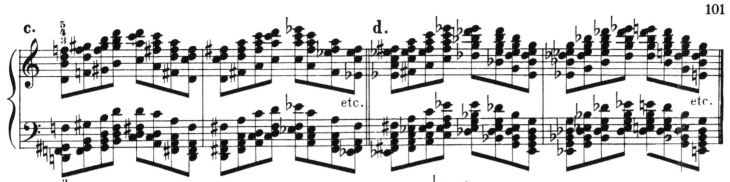

102

l. h. two octaves lower. _ l. h. zwei Octaven tiefer.

16268

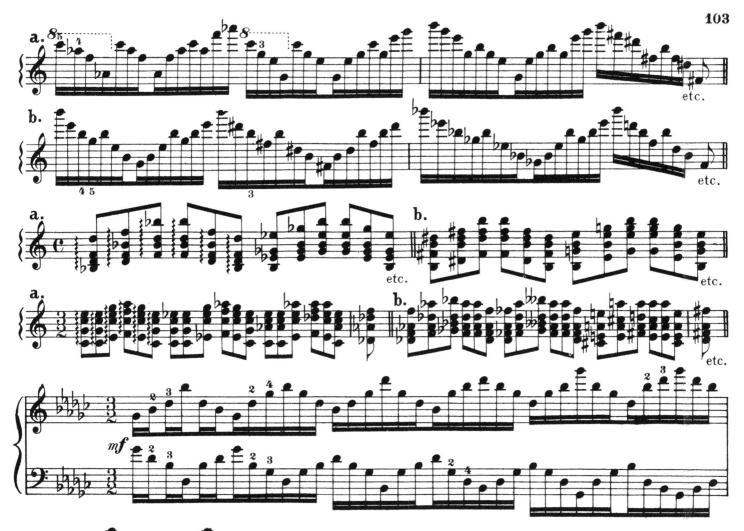

22.

Stretches.
Right hand alone. Rechte Hand allein.
Slowly. *Langsam.*

I.

Spannübungen.

Left hand alone. Linke Hand allein.

Allegro moderato.

Slowly. *Langsam.*

a.

*) With a free, easy movement of the elbow.
**) Each finger held down.

*) Mit freier, leichter Bewegung des Ellbogens.
**) Jeden Finger liegen lassen.

Allegro.

Moderato.

16268

a.

b.

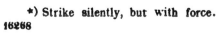

*) Strike silently, but with force.   *) Lautlos doch kräftig anzuschlagen.

legato

etc.

Moderato.

f

p leggiero

f

p

f

p

f

p

Left hand two octaves lower. Linke Hand zwei Octaven tiefer.

a.

etc.

etc.

16268 *) As before.   *) Wie vorher.

II.

Allegro.

Allegro.

leggiero

etc.

Through all the keys. Durch alle Tonarten.

ten.   *ten.*

leggiero

etc.

ten.   *ten.*

Allegro moderato.

legato

etc.

Allegro non troppo.

p legato

Ped.   *Ped.*   *Ped.*

Ped.

molto tranquillo

tranquillo

a. Allegro.

b. Moderato.

23.

Exercises in "piano" and "pianissimo".
Allegro.

„Piano" und „pianissimo" Übungen.

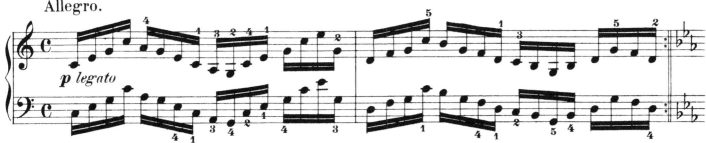

p legato

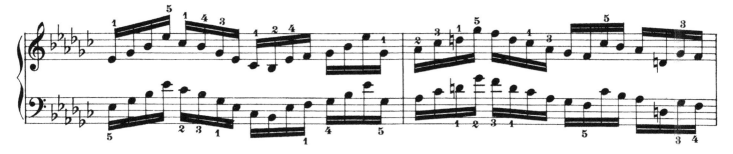

16268

Left hand two octaves lower.
Linke Hand zwei Octaven tiefer.

Presto.

p leggiero e non legato

Allegro moderato.

Allegro.

Allegro molto.

una corda

Rhythmical Studies.   Rhythmische Studien.

Moderato.

f legato

Through several major and minor keys.
Durch mehrere Dur und Moll Tonarten.

a. Allegro moderato.   b.

mf   p

etc.   mf

etc.

a.   b.   c.

etc.

Moderato.

f

p

a. Allegro.

b. *tranquillo*

Allegro.

Allegro.

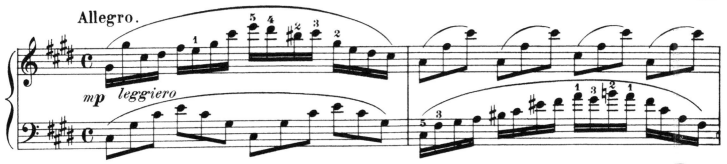

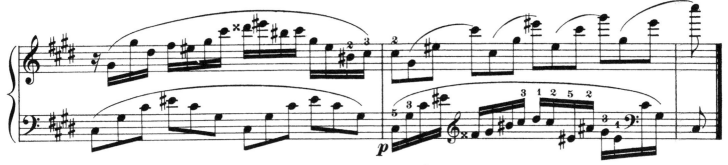

a. Allegro moderato.

Andante.

b.

c. Allegro.

Allegro molto.

Allegro.

Allegro vivace.

Allegro moderato.

Allegro.

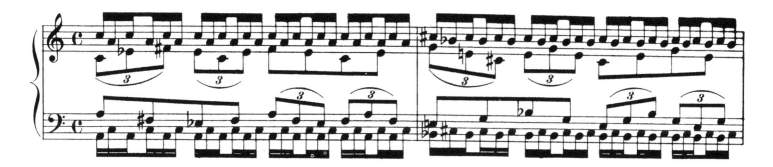

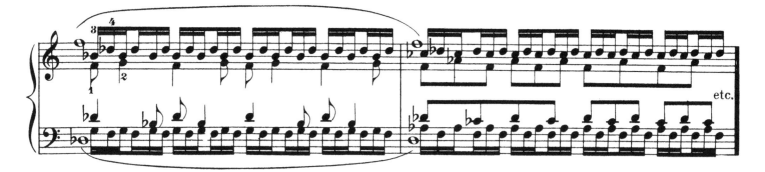

a.

b.

c. Moderato.

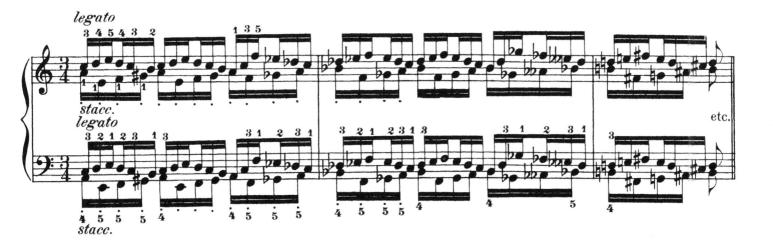

a. Moderato.

b.

a.

b.

a. Moderato.

b. Più mosso.

Allegro non troppo.

Through all the keys.
Durch alle Tonarten.

Moderato.
legato

Allegretto.

Andante.
legato

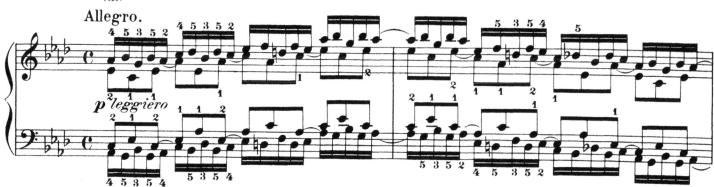

Allegro.

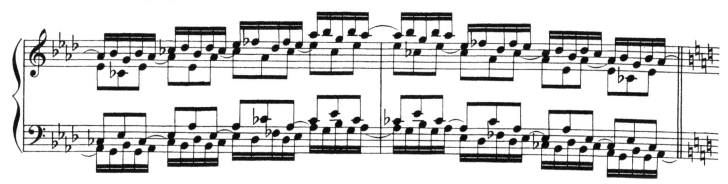

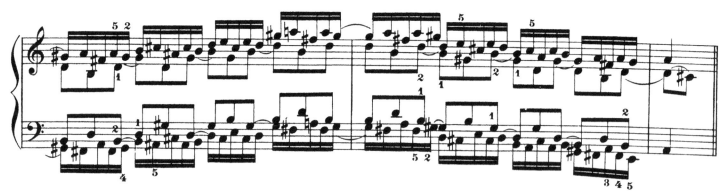

Allegro.

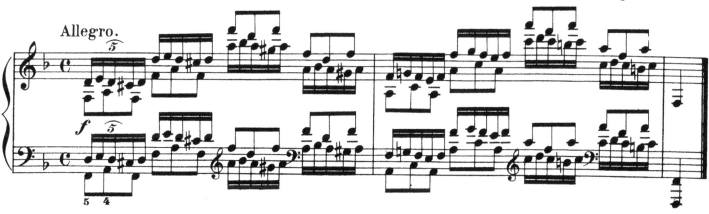